# EATING DISORDERS

T0020772

Corona Brezina

ROSEN
PUBLISHING

Published in 2024 by The Rosen Publishing Group, Inc.
2544 Clinton Street, Buffalo, NY 14224

First Edition

Editor: Greg Roza
Designer: Rachel Rising

Library of Congress Cataloging-in-Publication Data

Names: Brezina, Corona, author.
Title: Eating disorders / Corona Brezina.
Description: Buffalo : Rosen Publishing, [2024] | Series: @RosenTeenTalk |
  Includes bibliographical references and index.
Identifiers: LCCN 2023000009 (print) | LCCN 2023000010 (ebook) | ISBN
  9781499469011 (library binding) | ISBN 9781499469004 (paperback) | ISBN
  9781499469028 (ebook)
Subjects: LCSH: Eating disorders in adolescence--Juvenile literature.
Classification: LCC RJ506.E18 B76 2024  (print) | LCC RJ506.E18  (ebook) |
  DDC 616.85/2600835--dc23/eng/20230125
LC record available at https://lccn.loc.gov/2023000009
LC ebook record available at https://lccn.loc.gov/2023000010

Manufactured in the United States of America

CPSIA Compliance Information: Batch #CSPK24. For Further Information contact Rosen Publishing at 1-800-237-9932.

Find us on

# CONTENTS

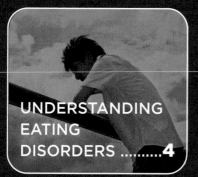

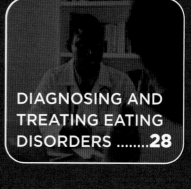

# Chapter 1

# Understanding Eating Disorders

I got onto the swim team my sophomore year! I'd worked so hard to prepare for tryouts. But then I started to worry. All the other guys looked fitter than me. I felt like I was skinny and weak.

One night, I was too worried to sleep. I went downstairs for a bite to eat. Then I couldn't stop eating. It was as if I completely lost control. I felt awful about myself afterward.

Then it happened again and again. My friends asked why I was acting so down. I was too **ashamed** to tell the truth.

My mother dragged me to the doctor. He said that I might have **binge** eating disorder (BED). I didn't know guys could get eating disorders!

Jacob's story isn't rare. Many kids his age have similar problems with food as they grow up. The good news is, there is help out there.

# FOOD ISSUES

Eating disorders are serious **mental** health conditions. People with eating disorders have issues with food and eating. They have unhealthy patterns of thinking about food. They also have problems with their eating habits. They may eat too much food or too little food. Eating disorders often start when someone goes on a diet.

Eating disorders can be difficult to treat. But many people successfully recover, or get better.

Eating disorders are mental health disorders that can also affect physical (or bodily) health. This can be from lack of **nutrition** or the result of harmful eating habits.

# Addressing the Problem

It's important to get **treatment** for an eating disorder. Early treatment makes recovery more likely. However, reports show that eight out of ten people don't seek treatment.

in this age group have

**Eating disorder** - NO

/'iːtɪn dɪs ɔː(r)də(r)/

## DIFFERENT DISORDERS

Common eating disorders are anorexia nervosa, bulimia nervosa, and binge eating disorder (BED). These are covered later in the book. However, there are several less common eating disorders.

- Pica: Eating things that aren't food, such as dirt, hair, paper, or paint chips.

- Rumination: Repeatedly spitting up and re-chewing food.

- Avoidant/restrictive food intake disorder (ARFID): Avoidance of (staying away from) many kinds of food, which causes health problems.

- Other specified feeding and eating disorder (OSFED): An eating disorder that doesn't fit under other disorders.

# ANOREXIA NERVOSA

People with anorexia nervosa are **obsessed** with being thin. They eat very little food. They often exercise a lot. They might think about food all the time. But even when they're very skinny, they think they're fat when they look in a mirror.

Someone with anorexia may weigh themselves several times a day. They're very scared by the idea that they could gain weight, even when they're dangerously thin.

A person with anorexia may also experience other issues. They may be **depressed** or **anxious**. Anorexia also causes serious physical health problems. It affects the heart, blood, bones, and the **digestive system**. Recovery from **severe** anorexia can take a long time.

# Who Gets Anorexia?

Anorexia is most common in young women from 12 years old to 25.

Both men and women can live with anorexia.

Older adults can have anorexia too.

## A DANGEROUS DISORDER

Anorexia is a very serious disease, or illness. Anorexia can lead to death if it is not treated. The disease damages many different systems of the body. Patients might die from heart problems caused by anorexia, for example. People living with anorexia are at a higher risk of **suicide**.

If you or someone you know is having thoughts of suicide, it's important to know help is available 24/7 by calling or texting 988, the Suicide and Crisis Lifeline.

# BULIMIA NERVOSA

A person with bulimia sometimes eats a lot of food in a short amount of time. Then they make themselves purge. This means that they get rid of the food they ate. They may force themselves to vomit, or throw up. Sometimes they do extra exercise after eating. Or they may fast. They are often worried about their weight.

People with bulimia feel like their eating is out of control. They feel bad afterwards. They keep their problem a secret from others.

A person with bulimia may have puffy cheeks. This is possibly caused by glands near the mouth becoming swollen after frequent vomiting. A gland is a part of the body that makes substances that other parts of the body need.

# Ancient Bulimia

The ancient Egyptians practiced throwing up after eating. They thought it could be good for health by preventing diseases that can come from food.

# Health Effects of Bulimia

Serious digestive problems

An imbalance of **minerals** in the body such as sodium and calcium

Stomach acid causes tooth damage from frequent vomiting

# OVERCOMING BULIMIA

Even famous people can struggle with bulimia. Here are a few celebrities who have talked about living with this eating disorder:

- *American Idol* winner Kelly Clarkson
- Singer Elton John
- Reality TV star Sharon Osbourne
- Singer Lady Gaga ⟶

# BINGE EATING DISORDER

Binging means to eat unusually big amounts of food. People with binge eating disorder (BED) eat even though they're not hungry. They eat until they feel too full. They eat their food very fast. They often binge alone because they feel ashamed. Usually, a binge lasts a short time and can happen about every two hours.

People with BED may have weight problems. They're at risk of being obese, or very overweight. They may feel like they can't stop eating even when they are uncomfortably full. It might be hard for them to lose weight.

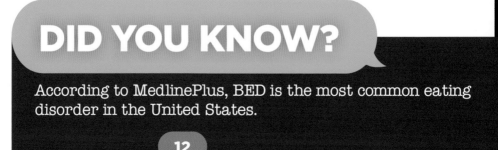

## DID YOU KNOW?

According to MedlinePlus, BED is the most common eating disorder in the United States.

# Orthorexia Nervosa

Orthorexia is a rare eating disorder. Someone with orthorexia is obsessed with eating only healthy foods. They may avoid any food that isn't natural.

## Finding Help

Check out the National Eating Disorders Association (NEDA) (nationaleatingdisorders.org/) for **resources** about eating disorders. They have a helpline too: (800) 931-2237. You can call, chat, or text if you need support. NEDA also raises awareness and supports research into, or the study of, eating disorders.

People who are obese are at a higher risk of BED. According to WebMD, about 10 to 15 percent of people who are mildly obese and who have tried to lose weight have BED.

# WHAT CAUSES EATING DISORDERS?

Many different **factors** cause eating disorders. Mental health problems are one factor. People with eating disorders often have low self-esteem. Or they may live with another mental illness such as depression.

Social factors can make someone feel pressured about their body. Family, friends, or the media might make a person believe that they should be thinner.

An eating disorder is sometimes linked to genetics. That means it is passed from parent to child. Someone who has a sister, brother, or other family member with an eating disorder is more likely to have one too.

# Trauma and Eating Disorders

**Trauma** is caused by difficult life events. People have trouble coping after living through trauma. Trauma has been linked to a higher likelihood of eating disorders. After trauma, people feel like they can't control their own lives. They may try to cope by binging or withholding food.

People sometimes blame themselves for their eating disorder. But it's nobody's fault—eating disorders aren't caused by the person with the disorder or by their family.

## POSITIVE THINKING

Self-esteem is how people sees themselves as a person. Poor body image can lower self-esteem. People who like and accept their body often have higher self-esteem.

# EATING DISORDERS AND BODY IMAGE

Body image is how a person thinks of their appearance, or the way they look. Many people with eating disorders have a poor body image. Girls may think they're too fat. Guys may believe that their muscles aren't big enough. Often, people with eating disorders have a **distorted** view of their bodies. They may think they are too fat even if they are underweight.

Someone with an eating disorder may talk about how they dislike how they look. They might wear baggy clothes to hide their body.

# Reading Recommendation

Laurie Halse Anderson wrote the novel *Wintergirls*. It's about a pair of high school girls with eating disorders. The story describes many of the treatments that teens can turn to when eating disorders **threaten** their lives.

A poor body image can lead to eating disorders such as anorexia and bulimia. People with a poor body image are also more likely to experience depression and low self-esteem.

# UNREALISTIC STANDARDS

Society and the media send the message that certain body types are more attractive or acceptable. Here are some examples:

- Characters seen in movies and on TV are usually thinner, fitter, and more attractive than ordinary people.

- Barbie dolls are unrealistically thin.

- Action figures such as superheroes have impossibly large muscles.

# RISK FACTORS

Common risk factors are found in many people with eating disorders. They tend to diet. Some people with eating disorders were bullied. They were sometimes targeted about their weight. Big life changes can help trigger, or cause, an eating disorder.

Certain activities are linked to eating disorders. People involved in some sports are at a higher risk. Examples include wrestling, gymnastics, figure skating, and swimming. Athletes may feel pressured, or pushed, to keep their weight down. Activities such as theater and modeling are also risk factors.

Cases of eating disorders increased during the COVID-19 **pandemic**. The National Eating Disorders Association (NEDA) saw a huge increase in calls from March 2020 to October 2021.

# WHO GETS EATING DISORDERS?

Anybody can have an eating disorder. This includes people of all ages, races, and genders. Women are more likely to have eating disorders. But men can have them too. LGBTQ+ youth are at a higher risk than their peers. Both low-income and wealthy people can have eating disorders.

People with an eating disorder can be underweight, overweight, or average size. You can't tell by appearance if a person has an eating disorder.

Anyone can struggle with an eating disorder. Some people fail to seek treatment because they have the wrong idea that only certain types of people get eating disorders.

# EATING DISORDERS AND AGE

According to the National Institute of Mental Health (NIMH), a common medium age for anorexia and bulimia to start is 18 years old. A common medium age for BED to start is 21 years old. But people can have eating disorders later in life. Some people deal with eating disorders for years. Others develop them as older adults. These are called late-onset eating disorders.

# Chapter 3

# Symptoms of Eating Disorders

I was always a skinny kid. But in middle school, my body changed. I hated it. I tried to go on a diet. But I was hungry all the time.

One day, I got home from school and ate a whole pack of cookies. I couldn't help myself. I felt so bad that I made myself throw up. I started doing it more often.

Sometimes, I got really stressed. Purging would make me feel better.

I was finally caught at it in the school bathroom. My friend Bella was standing outside the stall. I waited for her to tell me how gross I was. Instead, she took my hand.

"Please, come with me to the nurse's office," she said gently. "You need help."

# KNOW THE SIGNS

People with eating disorders have issues, or problems, with food. They often hide their problems. But there are signs that something's wrong. They may try out fad diets. They might obsess over what they eat. People with bulimia or BED often eat in secret. People with anorexia may be very thin.

There are **emotional** signs too. Someone with an eating disorder may have mood swings. They may feel depressed. They might lose interest in activities they always liked. They may push away their friends.

Check out the National Association of Anorexia Nervosa and Associated Disorders (ANAD) (anad.org/) to connect with other people struggling with eating disorders. The association provides weekly online support groups for young people. It also provides resources for learning about eating disorders and getting help.

People with eating disorders often have odd eating habits. They may skip meals or obsess over what kinds of food they eat, or how much they eat.

# FOOD ISSUES

People with eating disorders may show odd eating habits. Here are some examples:

- Only eating one type of food

- Refusing to eat certain kinds of foods—but it can be healthy to follow a vegan (meat and dairy free) or vegetarian (meat-free) diet

- A dislike of eating around other people

- Skipping meals or eating very little

# HEALTH EFFECTS

Eating disorders can damage one's health in many ways. Anorexia and bulimia can cause heart problems. People with these disorders often have skin problems. Their hair and nails may be brittle and dry. People with anorexia may feel weak or dizzy. They may have a hard time paying attention.

Eating disorders cause long-term consequences, or effects. Purging can harm the digestive system. Anorexia can cause thinning of the bones. Women who had an eating disorder may have difficulty getting pregnant. Their babies may have health issues too someday.

Some patients with anorexia force themselves to lose so much weight that they're in danger of dying from starvation, or a lack of food.

# Medical Consequences of BED

Weight gain

Heart disease

Type II diabetes

## BEYOND THE BODY

The harm done by eating disorders goes beyond physical damage.

- Emotional health:
  - Eating disorders worsen mental health issues.
  - Poor nutrition can affect how the brain works and change people's **behavior.**

- Relationships with others:
  - People with eating disorders are afraid that their problem will be discovered, so they stay away from family and friends.
  - Eating disorders damage friendships and people with eating disorders start to feel lonely.

# Chapter 4

# DIAGNOSING AND TREATING EATING DISORDERS

Eating disorders are **diagnosed** by a doctor. The doctor will ask questions about medical history. They will perform a physical exam. They may order lab tests. A mental health worker may ask questions too.

There are specific **criteria** for each disorder. If a person matches many of the criteria, they will receive a diagnosis. An early diagnosis is helpful. Treatment is more likely to be effective. There is less danger of severe health consequences.

# Seeking Help

Check out **Psychology** *Today*. It's a magazine and website—find it at www.psychologytoday.com. It provides mental health resources that include information, or facts, about eating disorders. It also offers way to contact mental health professionals.

In order to diagnose an eating disorder, other possible medical conditions that could produce the signs and symptoms must be considered and ruled out.

# CRITERIA FOR EATING DISORDERS

Here are some examples of criteria used to diagnose eating disorders:

- Anorexia: Low body weight from not eating enough food
- Bulimia: Binging and purging at least weekly for three months
- BED: Frequently eating large amounts of food in a short amount of time, and feeling unable to control how much one is eating

# TREATING EATING DISORDERS WITH THERAPY

A team of medical professionals works together to help patients with eating disorders. Treatments aim to change how a patient eats and thinks about food. Most patients receive **therapy**. They talk to a **counselor** or psychologist about their problems. They may also receive group therapy and family therapy.

Therapy can address much more than a patient's eating disorders. Therapy helps them change their thinking and behavior. The patient can learn healthy eating habits.

# Cognitive Behavioral Therapy (CBT)

There are many helpful approaches to treating eating disorders. One common type of therapy is cognitive behavioral therapy (CBT). Cognitive means having to do with mental activities (thinking, remembering, learning, etc.). Patients learn about their unhealthy patterns of thinking. They replace them with healthier thoughts and behaviors.

Cognitive behavioral therapy often involves keeping a diary. This helps people identify triggers that cause unhealthy eating behaviors and replace them with new habits.

**Myth:**

Someone can get over an eating disorder if they just make up their mind to eat right.

**FACT:**

Eating disorders are serious medical conditions. A person's eating disorder is an attempt to cope with deeper problems. They must address mental health issues in order to recover.

# MEDICAL TREATMENT FOR EATING DISORDERS

Eating disorders can cause health problems. Patients may need medical treatment to address these issues. They may also have mental health conditions. Some patients are considered at risk of harming themselves.

People with eating disorders may spend time in hospitals or clinics. For example, people with anorexia may be severely underweight. They may need a feeding tube to restore weight at first. Then they'll take control of their own eating. Later, they will address mental health issues while moving past their eating disorder. People with bulimia may also require hospital treatment.

# Levels of Care

Outpatient treatment: Regularly scheduled treatment meetings

Partial hospitalization treatment: Spending most days receiving treatment

Residential treatment: Living in a hospital or clinic setting to receive treatment

Inpatient treatment: Receiving care from a treatment team at a hospital for severe physical and mental illness

## WHAT CAN YOU DO TO HELP A FRIEND?

- Let them know that you're concerned.
- Don't blame them for their problem or judge them.
- Don't comment on their weight or appearance.
- Urge them to seek help.
- Provide support as they recover.

Medical treatment programs for eating disorders address health issues, provide therapy, and work toward nutrition goals. Patients may also receive medications, or drugs.

# Mia's Anorexia

My family tried hard to help me through my
rexia, but nothing worked. I kept losing weight.
ally, I went to a clinic for eating disorders.

A medical team tracked my progress. They mac
see that I was being controlled by anorexia. My
ng disorder wasn't really about weight. The root
in my thinking. I could change my thinking to
rge of my health.

My family and friends helped me so much. I
ized how much they cared about me as a person
ey never thought my appearance was important.

Now I'm working to **maintain** my recovery.
metimes I'm afraid that I'm going to relapse, but
ned helpful coping skills. I think I can maintain
lth and enjoy food again.

The word "relapse" means to fall back into a f
worse state. It takes effort to stay healthy and
relapsing back into unhealthy eating habits.

# NUTRITIONAL COUNSELING

Patients with eating disorders need to change how they think about food. A dietitian is a professional who teaches about healthy eating. They set a healthy target weight. They also teach basic facts about nutrition and planning meals. The goal is to make balanced eating habits normal.

Each patient has unique needs. People with anorexia may aim to restore a healthy weight. People with bulimia may learn to keep up regular eating patterns. Patients also learn about healthy movement. Good nutrition is necessary to fuel physical activity.

Patients learn about intuitive eating, which means paying attention to the body's cues in deciding what to eat or recognizing feelings such as hunger or fullness.

# CAN MEDICATIONS HELP?

Many medications used to treat other mental health conditions can be effective in treating eating disorders. This is because they can help people control their thoughts and behaviors.

Antidepressants are the drug type most commonly given to people with eating disorders, usually binge eating disorder and bulimia. They don't affect patients' weight. Instead, they change how the brain works. They help treat anxiety and depression too. Many people with eating disorders also often live with these conditions. Medications often work best if patients take them for weeks or months.

# Family Involvement

Family support is very important for someone struggling with an eating disorder. Parents can help their teens change their eating habits. Mental health professionals can provide information and help for the whole family.

Treatment plans for eating disorders often combine several different approaches. Medications along with therapy can improve patients' chances of recovery.

## RESOURCES FOR TEENS

Check out workbooks that help you address your eating disorder issues. A good place to start is *8 Keys to Recovery from an Eating Disorder Workbook* by Carolyn Costin and Gwen Schubert Grabb. The authors share their own stories about eating disorder recovery. Teens learn to cope through activities such as journaling, setting goals, and self-reflection.

# Chapter 5

# RECOVERING FROM AN EATING DISORDER

Eating disorders can be difficult to treat. Patients may relapse after successful treatment. This means that they start having problems with eating again. Relapse is especially likely when they're feeling stressed. They may need more treatment.

Some patients only achieve a partial recovery. This means they still show some symptoms of an eating disorder. A person with anorexia may reach a healthy weight, for example, but they may still have a poor body image or bad eating habits. They are at a higher risk of relapse.

# Recommended Reading

Jenni Schaefer wrote a best-selling book about her recovery from an eating disorder called *Life Without Ed: How One Woman Declared Independence from Her Eating Disorder and How You Can Too.*

A patient is considered recovered if they no longer show symptoms that fit the criteria for an eating disorder. They also must have an overall healthy view of food, body weight, and self-image.

## RECOGNIZING RECOVERY

- Physical: Healthy weight

- Behavioral: Normal eating habits

- Psychological: • Good body image and self-esteem
  • No anxiety about weight or appearance

# PREVENTING EATING DISORDERS

Is it possible to keep eating disorders from happening? Some groups are trying to address the issue. Many mental health groups provide education and resources about eating disorders. They can be found online. The National Institute of Mental Health (nimh.nih.gov), for example, is a government agency. It supports research on mental health, including eating disorders.

Modern **activism** movements talk about body positivity too. They stress the acceptance of all body types.

self love

find the good
not the bad

you are beautiful

free    Body positive    be happy

positive self talk    don't judge

be humble    respect for others

don't compare    show love

# Seeking Support

The Jed Foundation provides a wealth of mental health resources. Find it at jedfoundation.org. The site offers information on mental health conditions, including eating disorders. It also provides guidance on helping friends through difficult situations.

The body-positivity movement aims to prevent people from being unhappy with their bodies, which leads to poor self-esteem.

## AVOIDING RELAPSE

- Plan to avoid certain places, people, or habits (triggers) linked to an eating disorder.

- Seek help or talk to a friend if you're feeling you are at risk of relapse.

- Limit social media use to avoid too many unhealthy messages about body shape and eating habits.

# Jacob Overcomes BED

My doctor sent me to a **psychiatrist**. She'd treated many other patients with binge eating disorder. BED is one of the most common eating disorders for guys. She taught me ways to stop obsessing over my body image issues. She also ordered an antidepressant for my anxiety.

A couple of my teammates told me that they also sometimes felt bad about their bodies. It was good to know that I'm not alone.

My coach was very supportive too. He told me that body shape and muscles aren't the most important traits for success as an athlete. What really matters are inner qualities like motivation and grit.

I'm feeling much better about myself! I'm able to focus on, or pay more attention to, school and swimming again. I can't wait until next season.

# GLOSSARY

**activism:** Acting strongly in support of or against an issue.

**anxious:** Feeling afraid, worried, or nervous about something that might happen. Anxiety is a fear about something that might happen. If it doesn't go away and keeps getting worse, it can lead to an anxiety disorder.

**ashamed:** Feeling guilt or shame.

**behavior:** The way someone acts.

**binge:** To eat or drink too much in a short time period.

**counselor:** Someone who helps others with emotional pain, improving self-esteem, and carrying out positive behavioral changes.

**criterion:** A mark or trait that characterizes something. The plural is criteria.

**depressed:** Feeling sad, or affected by the serious mental health condition depression.

**diagnose:** To identify a disease by its signs and symptoms.

**digestive system:** A body system that is involved in digesting and absorbing food, in addition to getting rid of waste.

**distort:** To twist or change the true meaning of something, or to make something seem false or unnatural.

**emotional:** Relating to emotions, or strong feelings such as anger, joy, and love.

**factor:** Something that can cause something else to happen.

**maintain:** To care for something by making repairs and changes when needed.

**mental:** Having to do with the mind.

**mineral:** A substance that is important in small quantities for the nutrition of people and animals.

**nutrition:** The food that living things need to survive and how it affects their health.

**obsess:** To think or talk about something too much.

**pandemic:** An illness that affects many people in a large geographic area, such as multiple countries.

**psychiatrist:** A medical doctor who diagnoses and treats emotional, mental and behavioral conditions.

**psychology:** A science that centers on the study of the mind and behaviors. A psychologist is a specialist who studies the mind in addition to treating behavioral, emotional, and mental health conditions.

**resource:** Something that can be used.

**severe:** Very bad or serious.

**suicide:** The act of killing oneself.

**therapy:** A way of dealing with problems that makes people's bodies and minds feel better.

**threaten:** To cause someone to feel insecure or afraid.

**trauma:** An experience that causes serious distress.

**treatment:** A way of dealing with a medical problem.

# INDEX